THE SUN & MOON SIGNS LIBRARY

ARIES

21 MARCH – 20 APRIL

JULIA AND DEREK PARKER

Photography by Monique le Luhandre

Illustrations by Danuta Mayer

DK

DORLING KINDERSLEY

London • New York • Stuttgart

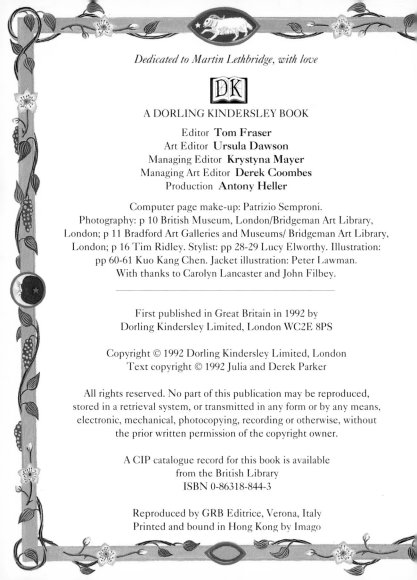

Dedicated to Martin Lethbridge, with love

DK

A DORLING KINDERSLEY BOOK

Editor **Tom Fraser**
Art Editor **Ursula Dawson**
Managing Editor **Krystyna Mayer**
Managing Art Editor **Derek Coombes**
Production **Antony Heller**

Computer page make-up: Patrizio Semproni.
Photography: p 10 British Museum, London/Bridgeman Art Library,
London; p 11 Bradford Art Galleries and Museums/ Bridgeman Art Library,
London; p 16 Tim Ridley. Stylist: pp 28-29 Lucy Elworthy. Illustration:
pp 60-61 Kuo Kang Chen. Jacket illustration: Peter Lawman.
With thanks to Carolyn Lancaster and John Filbey.

First published in Great Britain in 1992 by
Dorling Kindersley Limited, London WC2E 8PS

A CIP catalogue record for this book is available
from the British Library
ISBN 0-86318-844-3

Reproduced by GRB Editrice, Verona, Italy
Printed and bound in Hong Kong by Imago

CONTENTS

INTRODUCING
ARIES

ARIES, THE SIGN OF THE RAM, IS THE FIRST SIGN OF THE
ZODIAC. ON OR AROUND 21 MARCH THE SUN MOVES
INTO ARIES, MARKING THE START OF THE ASTROLOGICAL
NEW YEAR, ASTROLOGY'S NEW YEAR'S DAY.

Ariens have a psychological need to win, and to stand out from the crowd, ahead of all other competition. Here is assertiveness, self-assurance, and an uncomplicated approach to life. In order to achieve their goals, Ariens will strip away everything that is unnecessary to them. Here too is lively enthusiasm and an abundance of physical energy.

Traditional groupings

As you read through this book you will come across references to the elements and the qualities, and to positive and negative, or masculine and feminine signs.

The first of these groupings, that of the elements, comprises fire, earth, air, and water signs. The second, that of the qualities, divides the Zodiac into cardinal, fixed, and mutable signs. The final grouping is made up of positive and negative, or masculine and feminine signs. Each Zodiac sign is associated with a combination of components from these groupings, all of which contribute different characteristics to it.

Arien characteristics

The Arien element is fire – a bright, crackling inner fire that is easily ignited. Ariens must do all that they possibly can to keep this fire alive, for if it vanishes, great potential is lost, enthusiasm dies, and inner fulfilment is sure to be lacking. The sign belongs to the cardinal quality, which makes Ariens outgoing in manner. It is a positive, masculine sign, and therefore its subjects are inclined towards extroversion.

The traditional colour of Aries is red, although blue is sometimes suggested, and its ruling planet is the red planet, Mars. Ariens are easily roused to anger, but once they have expressed their feelings, they bear neither malice nor resentment.

ARIES PISCES AQUARIUS CAPRICORN SAGITTARIUS SCORPIO LIBRA VIRGO LEO CANCER GEMINI TAURUS

The Zodiac Wheel

The relationship between each Zodiac sign and the traditional astrological groupings is made clear within the Zodiac wheel. As you read through this book you will also discover references to polar, or opposite signs, and these, too, can be easily worked out by referring to the wheel.

FIRE

CARDINAL   EARTH

MASCULINE MUTABLE   AIR

FEMININE   FIXED   WATER

MYTHS & LEGENDS

THE ZODIAC, WHICH IS SAID TO HAVE ORIGINATED IN BABYLON
AS LONG AS 2,500 YEARS AGO, IS A CIRCLE
OF CONSTELLATIONS THROUGH WHICH THE SUN MOVES
DURING THE COURSE OF A YEAR.

The Ram is not shown in the earliest, Babylonian Zodiacs, and probably first appeared in the charts drawn up by Ancient Egyptian astronomers. It can be seen on the walls of the temple of the Egyptian Pharaoh, Ramesses the Great, near the Valley of the Kings in Thebes.

The Golden Fleece

In the complicated legend of the golden ram, the Ancient Greeks continued to foster the mythical associations of the creature.

Babylonian votive ram
Since the earliest times, imagery associated with the ram has appeared in the devotional art of many different cultures.

Without elaborating upon the many characters involved, the story is basically as follows. Phrixus and his sister, Helle, the children of the Boeotian King Athamas, were quietly walking in a wood one day when they met their mother, Nephele, leading a fine golden ram by the horns. She claimed that Poseidon, the god of the sea, had changed the beautiful Theophane, daughter of Bisaltes, into a ewe and himself into a ram, the better to court her. Nephele's ram was their child. She ordered Phrixus and Helle to ride him to the kingdom of Colchis, by the Black Sea,

Jason steals the Golden Fleece

This painting by Herbert Draper (1864 – 1920) shows Jason escaping from Colchis. To delay their pursuers, Medea, the king of Colchis's daughter, who had fallen in love with Jason, threw her brother's body into the sea.

and sacrifice him to Ares, the god of war. This they did, and the ram's golden fleece was hung in the temple of Ares at Colchis, where it was guarded by a dragon that never slept.

Many years later, Jason, rightful king of Iolcus in Thessaly, could only claim his throne if he recovered the Golden Fleece. He led the Argonauts, a group of heroes, to Colchis, where, after performing a number of apparently impossible tasks, he took not only the Fleece but

also Medea, the king of Colchis's daughter. In fact, if it had not been for Medea's assistance in delaying her father's pursuit, Jason could well have been unable to make good his escape. Following his triumphant return, Jason mounted the throne and reigned happily ever after.

Jason's story embodies many of the qualities that are traditionally associated with Ariens: courage, an adventurous spirit, energy, and the need to win out over adversity.

ARIES
SYMBOLISM

CERTAIN HERBS, SPICES, FLOWERS, TREES, GEMS, METALS, AND
ANIMALS HAVE LONG BEEN ASSOCIATED WITH PARTICULAR
ZODIAC SIGNS. SOME ASSOCIATIONS ARE SIMPLY FUN, WHILE
OTHERS CAN BE USEFUL, FOR INSTANCE IN MEDICINE.

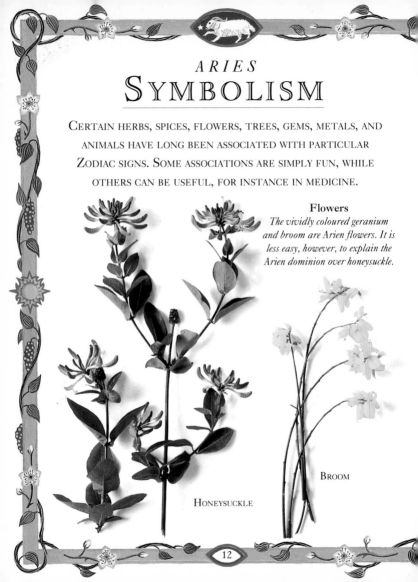

Flowers
*The vividly coloured geranium
and broom are Arien flowers. It is
less easy, however, to explain the
Arien dominion over honeysuckle.*

BROOM

HONEYSUCKLE

Trees
*Because of their prickly nature,
all thorn-bearing trees and shrubs
are dominated by Aries.*

MUSTARD POWDER   CAYENNE PEPPER

HAWTHORN

Spices
*Aries is a fire sign, and is therefore said to
rule cayenne pepper. The same is true of
mustard and tartly flavoured capers.*

PEPPERMINT

HOLLY

Herbs
*Peppermint, which is said to
ease digestive complaints when
brewed as a tea, has long been
associated with Aries.*

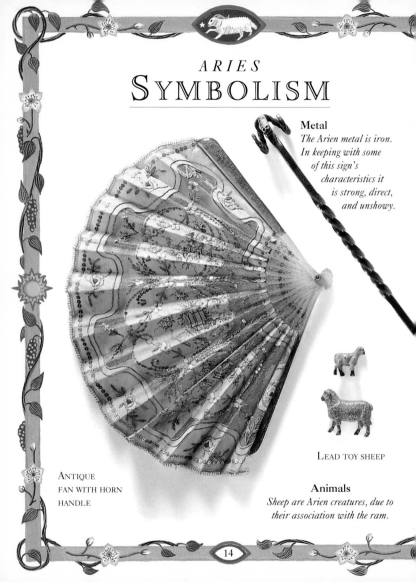

ARIES
SYMBOLISM

Metal
The Arien metal is iron. In keeping with some of this sign's characteristics it is strong, direct, and unshowy.

LEAD TOY SHEEP

ANTIQUE
FAN WITH HORN
HANDLE

Animals
Sheep are Arien creatures, due to their association with the ram.

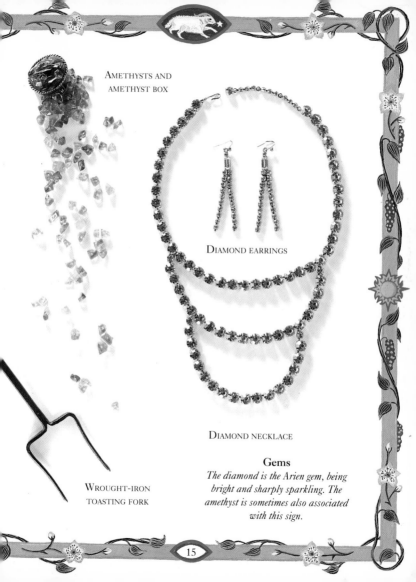

AMETHYSTS AND
AMETHYST BOX

DIAMOND EARRINGS

DIAMOND NECKLACE

WROUGHT-IRON
TOASTING FORK

Gems
The diamond is the Arien gem, being bright and sharply sparkling. The amethyst is sometimes also associated with this sign.

ARIES
PROFILE

THE OVERALL PHYSICAL APPEARANCE OF THE TYPICAL ARIEN IS
LIKELY TO REFLECT A SENSE OF IMMEDIACY. ARIENS
ARE OFTEN IN A HURRY, AND HAVE NO TIME TO WASTE ON
UNNECESSARY COMPLICATIONS.

The Arien stance is easily definable: it expresses confidence. You are likely to stand with your feet placed well apart, and your weight evenly distributed. Your gestures are probably rather uncomplicated – just like the normally straightforward Arien approach to life.

The body

When the Arien body is in good condition, it is very wiry, giving the general impression by the very way in which it moves that it is made of elastic. It is important that you keep yourself on the lean side, since if your body becomes sluggish so will your mind, and the whole pace of your life will slow down. Ariens often appear to lean forward when they walk. This

The Arien face

The Arien glyph is often visible in the line from the eyebrows to the nose.

could indicate that you are forever searching for your next challenge. It may also point to the fact that you have a tendency to jump forward in emergencies.

The face

Your hair is likely to be rather fine, or even flyaway. Male Ariens sometimes tend to lose their hair as they age and many of them have receding hairlines. The Arien forehead is typically broad and open, and the Arien glyph, ♈, can sometimes be seen in the line created by the eyebrows and the prominent nose. Your eyes no doubt betray your Arien sense of determination; they are very likely to be clear, alert, and often quick-moving. Many Ariens tend to possess very strong and characterful

The Arien stance

The Arien stance, which is very easy to recognize, is a very confident one. Your weight will be distributed very evenly.

chins that jut forward. You probably find it easy to break into a smile or a broad grin.

Style

Ariens like casual clothes, uncluttered by fussy details. At the same time, most people of this Sun sign possess the gift of always being able to look very stylish. Men look good in blazers and sweaters, women in well-matched separates. Clothes that restrict movement may not look appropriate, even on formal occasions. Ariens can spend quite a lot of money on their wardrobes. It could be that you enjoy wearing the most fashionable, very expensive tracksuits.

Many Ariens own favourite items of clothing with which they will not wish to be parted under any circumstances. This goes against their usual reluctance to be nostalgic.

In general

Ariens are always in a hurry. They take long, determined strides at a quick pace, and often barge through doors without too much concern for others who may be in their wake. As has already been mentioned, you may lean forward when you walk, and this could lead to you developing back problems at some time in your life. You should consciously try to hold yourself more upright, making sure that you keep your head up. In all, your rather robust approach to life will be reflected in the way that you act and dress.

ARIES
PERSONALITY

BECAUSE ARIES IS THE FIRST SIGN OF THE ZODIAC, THOSE BORN
WHILE THE SUN IS TRAVELLING THROUGH IT ARE NATURAL
LEADERS. THEY SHOULD BE ASSERTIVE, BUT NEVER RUTHLESS,
IN THEIR DEALINGS WITH OTHER PEOPLE.

Here is a Zodiac group that is positive and enthusiastic in its outlook. Ariens enjoy challenge, and should always have some important goals to achieve. You probably have a high physical energy level, and it is important that you express this positively and assertively. You can do this by developing a pacy lifestyle that is demanding both at work and in leisure. This will satisfy your Arien psychological motivation, which is to always win, and to be way out ahead of all your competitors.

At work
The straightforward Arien outlook on life is admirable: a daunting problem can be cut through in a matter of minutes. In fact, those of us who allow side issues to clutter up our attitudes and opinions could take lessons from Ariens. Of course, this can lead to the one real drawback of the Arien personality. In your determination to deal briskly with problems, you may all too easily over-simplify a situation. When working on complicated projects, Ariens should therefore preferably be able to confer with someone who can cope with the more detailed areas of the scheme.

Your attitudes
Your main vice is selfishness, and no matter how well adjusted you are, or what other planets provide counter-influences, this trait can emerge. It can nearly always be traced back to the "me first" syndrome. Self-awareness, and a little forethought when dealing with other people's feelings, will help enormously in overcoming this unpleasant tendency.

Many people of this sign have a tendency to take risks. If this side of their nature is controlled, and kept within certain limits, this becomes a positive adventurousness, which is, of course, marvellous. If it is not, the

Mars rules Aries

Mars, the Roman god of war, represents the ruling planet of Aries. The influence of Mars, which has a strong sexual emphasis, relates to the masculine side of an Arien's nature.

individual will sometimes act in a rather hot-headed or foolhardy manner, and learn the hard way.

The overall picture

The Arien energy level, both physical and emotional, is very high, and most Ariens make excellent use of it. Indeed, inner fulfilment will only come when you use your body and your mind like a single, well-adjusted and oiled machine.

This is one of the signs requiring a good measure of independence. Ariens do not suffer fools gladly, and you will make quite sure that you do things in your own way. Freedom of expression is important to you.

ARIES
ASPIRATIONS

WHATEVER THEIR CAREER, ARIENS ASPIRE TO REACH THE TOP
OF THE LADDER. YOU NEED CHALLENGE, AND MUST BE
ABLE TO EXPRESS YOURSELF THROUGH YOUR WORK. OF COURSE,
IT ALSO HAS TO INTEREST YOU.

Professional sport
*An above-average number of
professional sportsmen have a strong
Arien influence. Winning is important
to them, and it calls up all their
inherent energy.*

GUN-METAL
STOPWATCH

Motoring
*Cars can be a passion for Ariens.
Their natural exuberant haste
can, however, often
make them rather
impatient drivers.*

BRASS CAR HORN

1920s
MOTORING MAP

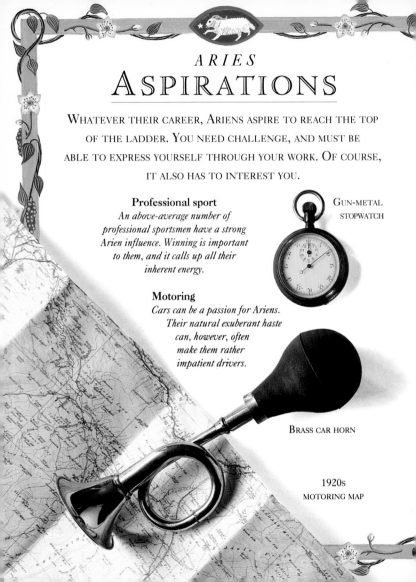

Engineering

Ariens of both sexes make good engineers and, in their spare time, are often enthusiastic amateur motor mechanics. They seem to positively enjoy getting their hands dirty.

1927 CIGARETTE CARDS DEPICTING ENGINEERING

PERSONAL MEDICAL IMPLEMENTS

Medicine

There is a traditional link between the medical profession and this sign. Perhaps because Aries rules the head, Ariens also make good psychiatrists.

DENTAL MOUTH MIRROR

Dentistry

Although Capricorn rules the teeth, Ariens are often drawn to working in the dental profession.

DENTAL PROBE

HORSE BRASS

Physical work

Arien energy is well suited to many different forms of physical activity, for example farming.

ARIES
HEALTH

FOR ARIENS TO KEEP WELL AND HEALTHY, THEY HAVE
TO BURN UP ENERGY THROUGH EXERCISE. IF YOUR
LIFESTYLE IS PHYSICALLY DEMANDING, IT WILL HELP YOU
TO STAY IN GOOD SHAPE.

The pioneering spirit of Aries is usually motivation enough to keep you moving, but at times when life lacks challenge, even the most energetic Arien will become lazy.

Your diet

Although you may like spicy foods, these are seldom good for Ariens. You will thrive on traditional, rather simple, dishes. Your diet may also benefit from being supplemented with the cell salt Potassium Phosphate (Kali. Phos.), which is thought to build brain cells, help prevent headaches, and alleviate depression.

Taking care

Ariens are not the most careful of Zodiac types and you will tend to cut and burn yourself rather more than is common. Therefore develop caution, especially when cooking or working with sharp tools. The Arien body area is the head, and it is true to say that Ariens either suffer badly from headaches – sometimes due to minor kidney disorders – or never have any. Ariens sometimes find it hard to modify an exercise regime. As you get older, this may lead to you damaging your body, and all of your old injuries may come back to plague you.

Italian red onions

Most strong-tasting foods, such as onions and leeks, are associated with Aries.

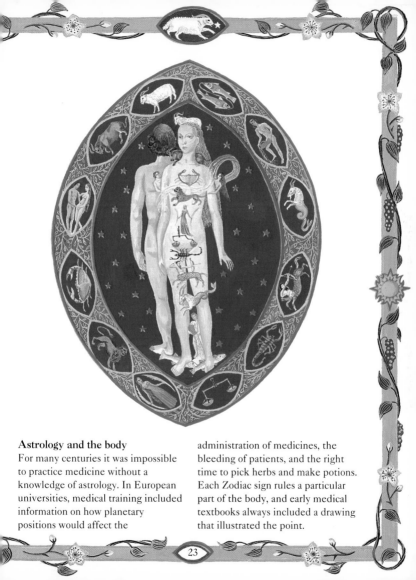

Astrology and the body

For many centuries it was impossible to practice medicine without a knowledge of astrology. In European universities, medical training included information on how planetary positions would affect the administration of medicines, the bleeding of patients, and the right time to pick herbs and make potions. Each Zodiac sign rules a particular part of the body, and early medical textbooks always included a drawing that illustrated the point.

ARIES AT
LEISURE

Each of the Sun signs traditionally suggests spare-time activities, hobbies, and holiday destinations. Although they are only suggestions, they often work out well, and are worth testing.

Travel

You will enjoy adventurous holidays, especially while you are young. Seeing the world will probably be more of a priority than comfort. Try England, Poland, France, Syria, and Palestine as holiday destinations.

VOLT
METER

POSTAGE STAMPS

Car maintenance

Ariens enjoy driving and maintaining their cars. The latter can, in fact, prove to be a lucrative hobby.

WALKING BOOTS

Horse-riding

You may enjoy pony trekking, and spending long days in the fresh air, irrespective of the weather.

HORSE'S BIT

Manual work
Iron is the metal of Mars, the planet that rules Aries. There is a long tradition that links Ariens with metalwork, tools, and machinery.

PAINT-STRIPPING TORCH

Mountaineering
The spirit of adventure possessed by many Ariens often attracts them to climbing and hill-walking.

1930s SPORTS CIGARETTE CARDS

Sport
Ariens need to exercise for both physical and psychological reasons. Football, hockey, and boxing are all possibilities. You will enjoy team games, especially if you are the captain.

ARIES IN
LOVE

BEING ONE OF THE MOST PASSIONATE SIGNS OF THE ZODIAC,
ARIENS FALL IN AND OUT OF LOVE VERY QUICKLY. A
TENDENCY TO SWEEP PROSPECTIVE PARTNERS OFF THEIR
FEET CAN, HOWEVER, END IN DISASTER.

You must learn to listen to your partner's needs, and ensure that selfishness does not spoil this wonderful sphere of life for you.

Pleasant romantic dinners and big nights out are sure to be part of the more mature Arien approach. When they are young, however, Ariens may seek what is wanted in the back seat of an old banger. All Ariens should ensure that their approach is not too gushing and fast for many people.

As a lover

Those partners on the receiving end of your admiration will no doubt find the experience both lively and enjoyable. In most cases, your enthusiasm is likely to be infectious, and the individual involved will find it both easy and pleasant to be swept up into a highly paced, sexually rewarding experience.

Types of Arien lover

Many Ariens have a beautifully poetic streak to their expression of love. This is something that one does not automatically expect to find in those who tend to rush things. However, Ariens must be aware of the possibility that once they are in love, an uncharacteristic

element of possessiveness may spoil their relationships. This type is, on the other hand, usually prone to be marvellously sensual and warm hearted. Some Ariens are marked by a light-hearted flirtatiousness, which can lead them towards duality and result in a great many awkward complications. Others will probably be so jealous of their independence that they will delay committing themselves to marriage until later than average. When in love, many Ariens enjoy surprising their partners. The small, and usually unexpected, gift will be presented quite frequently, and it is in winning ways such as this that they score highly. Many Ariens are considered to make excellent husbands and wives. They will, more often than not, encourage their spouses to express their potential in their own ways and, perhaps because they themselves have independent spirits, are extremely unlikely to create an unpleasant, claustrophobic atmosphere within any partnership. These particular Ariens should make sure that they do not choose partners who will attempt to inhibit their own positive and lively, energetic personalities.

ARIES AT
HOME

THE WARM AND WELCOMING ARIEN HOME IS COMFORTABLY,
SOLIDLY, AND UNFUSSILY FURNISHED. SHADES OF RED
ENHANCE THE FEELING OF WARMTH, AND THE BEDROOM,
IN PARTICULAR, HAS A VERY SENSUAL ATMOSPHERE.

Many Ariens enjoy spending time on improving their homes. They may, for example, replan their kitchens or gardens, and then do all of the work themselves. It is in fact the process of doing the work, rather than the end result, that provides real pleasure for an Arien.

You will probably prefer living near a busy street to setting up home in a peaceful rural setting. One important thing to consider is that as an Arien you will not want to be hemmed in or to feel restricted.

Furniture

Ariens tend to be rather careless, and hate anything insubstantial. You therefore generally choose durable

Candelabra
This candelabra has been made from the Arien metal, wrought iron.

furniture. Furthermore, having spent time choosing items, you are unlikely to want to waste more time, money, and energy searching for new items after only a couple of years. You must therefore make sure that you initially take your time when deciding to buy new pieces of furniture.

Soft furnishings

Ariens like their homes to have a warm, colourful glow. You probably enjoy creating an atmosphere that appears pleasing and informal to all who enter it.

Ariens are not usually very adventurous when it comes to choosing wallpaper, drapes, and curtains. You may well prefer plain,

Antique swords

Mars, the planet of war, rules Aries. It is therefore hardly surprising that many Ariens decorate their homes with weapons.

clear colours. Even though very young Ariens may be attracted to vivid or even garish designs (for duvet covers, for instance) this tendency usually diminishes as they age. By the time that they eventually feel ready to set up their own homes a certain restraint is likely to have emerged, which will make the final effect both interesting and tasteful.

Decorative objects

The decorative objects that Ariens enjoy owning reflect certain elements of the individual's personality. Your sexual energy may well be considerable, so reproductions of some famous erotic paintings could easily end up gracing your walls. Reproductions of paintings by the renowned Arien painter, Van Gogh, may also find a place in the Arien home. His energetic images of sunflowers sum up so much that is typical of the sign.

Mars, which is the planet of war, rules Aries, and the Arien metal is iron. You could therefore be the proud owner of some fine old weapons, for example antique swords or flint-lock pistols.

Armchair and cushions

The principle Arien colour is red, so there may be a good deal of it in your home. Ariens like solid, functional furniture.

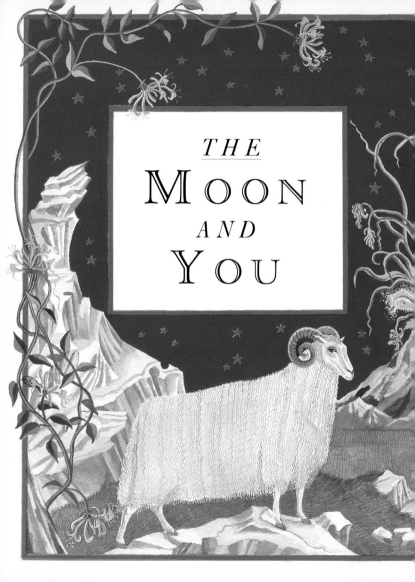

THE
MOON
AND
YOU

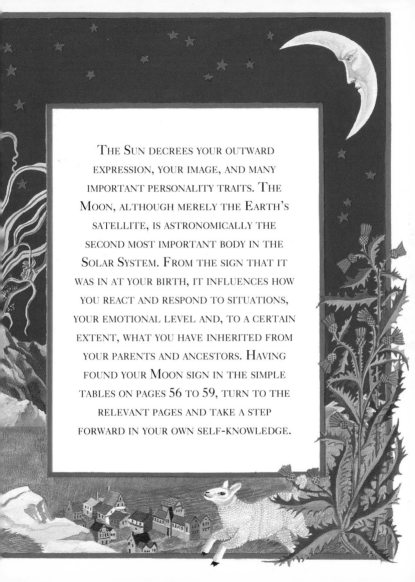

THE SUN DECREES YOUR OUTWARD
EXPRESSION, YOUR IMAGE, AND MANY
IMPORTANT PERSONALITY TRAITS. THE
MOON, ALTHOUGH MERELY THE EARTH'S
SATELLITE, IS ASTRONOMICALLY THE
SECOND MOST IMPORTANT BODY IN THE
SOLAR SYSTEM. FROM THE SIGN THAT IT
WAS IN AT YOUR BIRTH, IT INFLUENCES HOW
YOU REACT AND RESPOND TO SITUATIONS,
YOUR EMOTIONAL LEVEL AND, TO A CERTAIN
EXTENT, WHAT YOU HAVE INHERITED FROM
YOUR PARENTS AND ANCESTORS. HAVING
FOUND YOUR MOON SIGN IN THE SIMPLE
TABLES ON PAGES 56 TO 59, TURN TO THE
RELEVANT PAGES AND TAKE A STEP
FORWARD IN YOUR OWN SELF-KNOWLEDGE.

THE MOON IN
ARIES

WITH THE SUN AND MOON BOTH IN ARIES AT THE TIME OF YOUR
BIRTH, YOU WERE BORN UNDER A NEW MOON. ARIES IS A
FIRE SIGN, AND THIS ELEMENT POWERFULLY INFLUENCES YOUR
PERSONALITY AND REACTIONS.

Should you study a list of your Sun sign characteristics, you will probably recognize that a great many of them apply to you. Out of a list of perhaps 20 traits of a Sun sign listed in books or magazines, most people will strongly identify with 11 or 12. For you, however, the average increases considerably because the Sun and Moon were both in Aries when you were born.

Self-expression

Your Sun sign denotes fiery, positive emotion, and so does your Arien Moon. Obviously, with such a powerful force at your disposal, you will understand that it is essential for you to express your feelings, and to use your emotional energy positively. Do not bluster about, or flare up unnecessarily: learn to control your emotional energy, and use it evenly and constructively. Your Sun sign makes you assertive and your Moon

sign emphasizes this as your main motivation. You should also be aware that you may be terribly prone to hastiness, and could act prematurely.

Romance

The most serious Arien fault is selfishness and, more than for other people of your Sun sign, it could very easily mar your personal relationships. You can react to your partners in a self-centred way, putting your own interests first and ignoring their needs and suggestions. But once aware of the pitfalls of selfishness, you make a wonderful, passionate lover.

Your well-being

The effect of your Aries Moon on your health will be to increase your vulnerability to all Arien ailments. Most importantly, your inherent hastiness will incline you to be yet more accident-prone. The emotional intensity of your Moon underlines the

The Moon in Aries

likelihood of headaches. If they persist, it could be as the result of a mild kidney disorder, so arrange to have a medical check-up.

Self-control and the conscious awareness that you can overdo things are essential to your well-being.

Planning ahead

The Arien enterprising spirit will stand you in good stead when it comes to finance. Ariens are extremely decisive, but due to your

Arien Moon you may well react to situations without due thought. Be careful, for instance, when you invest, since mistakes can easily be made.

Parenthood

You will be a lively, enthusiastic parent, who will encourage your children in every area of their lives. But because you are so keen on your own interests, it may be all too easy for you to make the mistake of ignoring their individual tastes.

THE MOON IN
TAURUS

TAURUS IS AN EARTH SIGN, AND ITS QUALITIES ARE IN STRIKING
CONTRAST TO THOSE OF YOUR FIERY ARIEN SUN SIGN.
THEY WILL TEND TO MAKE YOU FAR LESS LIKELY TO EMBARK
ON UNWISE PREMATURE ACTIONS.

The qualities attributed to Aries and its neighbouring sign, Taurus, are totally opposite – so the fact that the Moon was in Taurus when you were born adds a very different dimension to your personality. If you are aware of these contrasting qualities, you will be able to express them without too much internal conflict.

Self-expression
Your Taurean Moon gives you an extremely useful tendency to react to situations both constructively and thoughtfully. You will not find it difficult to control a sense of urgency or hastiness, and will always want to think things through carefully.

Taurus and Aries are very much emotionally oriented signs, but you find it relatively easy to control your emotional flow and expression. At times, however, you will find it more difficult to throw off your anger than

many Ariens do. Be careful that a tendency leading towards resentment and brooding does not mar your admirably straightforward Arien approach to life.

Romance
Arien selfishness, coupled with a tendency to be possessive of your partner, can be a big stumbling block in an emotional relationship. Make sure that you use the affectionate, positive passion of your Moon to the full when responding to your partner. Allow the zest for love and sex that you obtain from your Aries Sun to colour your emotional relationships.

Your well-being
Taurus rules the throat, and at the first sign of a cold, you may well lose your voice and go down with a very sore throat. Many Ariens are wiry, but your Taurean Moon could add a lot of bulk to your frame. You may find it

The Moon in Taurus

extremely difficult to resist rich, sweet food. Weight gain could be a real problem for you.

Planning ahead
The Taurean business sense often beautifully compliments the Arien sense of enterprise. In fact, many people of your Sun sign are lucky enough to possess two different sources of income.

You have an extremely powerful intuitive streak when it comes to dealing with money, and will take fewer risks than many Ariens. Enterprise and good business sense, along with enthusiasm and a by no means sneaking regard for luxury, all go well together.

Parenthood
Arien enthusiasm will colour your attitude to your children, but you may sometimes find yourself being over-possessive. Watch out, too, for problems with the generation gap, as you can appear far more conventional to your children than you realize.

THE MOON IN
GEMINI

A COMBINATION OF ARIES (A FIRE SIGN) AND GEMINI (AN AIR
SIGN) WILL WHILE INCREASING ARIEN IMPATIENCE AND
RESTLESSNESS, GIVE YOU FAST RESPONSES TO SITUATIONS, A NEED
FOR IMMEDIATE ACTION, AND MANY BRIGHT IDEAS.

Fire and air blend well: Aries fire motivates you and colours your self-expression, while the airy Gemini Moon spurs you forward, keeps you alert, and ensures that you never waste a moment.

If your lifestyle is unrewarding, you will suffer much more than most Ariens. Avoid false starts, and the temptation to give up because you are bored. If you succeed in this, you will control what amounts to your most severe problem: a pathological hatred of boredom.

Self-expression
Although Arien directness is present in your personality, it is very easy for you to get side-tracked by the versatility that derives from your Moon sign. Allow the latter tendency some expression within the confines of a few well-chosen interests, and let it support a wider dimension within your career.

You may, perhaps, not entirely trust your powerful Arien emotions. Be very careful neither to suppress the expression of your feelings, nor, as you are more likely to do, simply to rationalize them out of existence.

Romance
You will possess plenty of Arien passion, and it will be obviously expressed through sex and other aspects of your emotional life. You are more than likely to be a good communicator, and will respond very fairly to your partner's desires and suggestions. Most fortunately, the inherent Arien selfish streak will be considerably mitigated in you.

Your well-being
The Geminian body areas are the hands and arms, so be extra careful that the Arien tendency to be accident-prone does not lead you to cut or burn them. Your Geminian

The Moon in Gemini

Moon may provoke periods of nervous tension. This, coupled with the Arien tendency to overdo things, and the need for a constant use of mental energy, could make relaxation rather difficult for you.

Planning ahead

In some spheres of your life, a cunning streak could combine with Arien selfishness and the desire to "be first". You will plan your every action, and will not be averse to scheming that will put you ahead of competitors. You will certainly voice your opinions, and your dynamic force will let you lead others skilfully.

Parenthood

You will make an extremely lively parent, and will find it very easy indeed to keep up with what your children are thinking, and with their various interests and crazes. In fact, it is you that could be the trendsetter, because your Geminian Moon instils in you a particularly strong interest in anything that is new and original.

THE MOON IN
CANCER

A COMBINATION OF THE FIRST ZODIAC FIRE SIGN (ARIES) AND THE
FIRST WATER SIGN (CANCER) BLENDS ASSERTIVE ENTHUSIASM
WITH AN INSTINCTIVE CARING, PROTECTIVE RESPONSE. IT WILL
ALSO HEIGHTEN YOUR EMOTIONAL LEVEL.

The tremendously high emotional content of your Sun and Moon combination is a vital key to your whole personality. As the Moon traditionally rules Cancer, its effect on you is even more powerful than it is on those who have it in another sign.

Self-expression
While Aries is extroverted, Cancer tends to be introverted, and you have some of the qualities of both. But there are areas where Aries and Cancer sympathize. Both signs are, for instance, of the cardinal quality, and share an important and expressive outgoing nature. You are generally forthcoming – Aries sees to that – but the Moon is also likely to make you tender, caring, and sympathetic.

Your Moon sign will probably make you somewhat apprehensive when challenged; it will make you intuitive, which is good, but it will also incline you to worry. Couple this with a powerful Cancerian imagination, and when something troubles you, you can easily begin to feel that your world has collapsed around you.

While much about the Cancer personality is soft and tender, there is, conversely, also a lot of toughness present, and this is very good when blended with more forthright, assertive Arien qualities.

Romance
You have the high, fiery passion of Aries plus the sensual, caring, and tender expression of love typical of Cancer. This is a pretty stunning combination, but you may find that you sometimes smother your partners with affection. Try not to be too sensitive, sentimental, or nostalgic.

Your well-being
You will work extremely hard, and could feel wound up at times; develop relaxation techniques to counter the

The Moon in Cancer

tendency. Most Ariens cope well with stress, but the Cancerian tendency to worry may stop you from taking as philosophical an attitude to problems as you otherwise might. Stress could also affect your digestion, so look carefully at your diet. It may be that you would benefit from eating far less spicy food.

Planning ahead

Your Cancerian Moon will, in general, make you marvellously and intelligently shrewd. This is especially true when it comes to business and finance. Follow your

powerful instincts, but do not let any fiery Arien enthusiasm entirely quench deep-rooted caution.

Parenthood

You will enjoy family life enormously, and may be eager to have children. But even though you will be an excellent and very lively parent, when your children want to leave home, you may find it hard to let them go. Right from the start, avoid an instinctive tendency to over-protect them. While you will want to give your children a happy home, beware of trying to make it too comfortable.

THE MOON IN
LEO

YOUR LIFE CAN OFTEN BE HECTIC BUT, BECAUSE YOU HAVE AN
INSTINCT FOR GETTING THINGS RIGHT, YOU WILL NOT BE
INCLINED TO TAKE SHORT CUTS TO ATTAIN YOUR GOALS. THIS
CAUTION WILL TEMPER UNDUE HASTE OR CARELESSNESS.

You possess very powerful feelings, and will enjoy expressing them, and your opinions, forcefully and to great effect.

Self-expression
Your Arien ability and motivation to win and to lead is enhanced by Leo's instinctive organizing ability. You should, can, and must aim to go far, but without hurting others. The chances are that with this combination you are a born leader, and if you achieve inner fulfilment, others will gladly follow your example.

You may tend to react in a somewhat pompous and bossy way at times and, if accused of this, your Arien Sun will encourage you to feel embarrassed. In fact, Aries is one of the least pompous of the 12 Zodiac signs. Therefore take heed: the influence from the Moon sign is powerful, and does influence the way other people react to us.

In anyone who has an influence from Leo, there is usually an urge for some form of creative expression. Ariens often love bright, vivid colours, so you may like to paint; but you will probably not be terribly patient. Do not, therefore, concern yourself with detail. Just slap the paint on liberally, and have fun, because the act of doing so can be very creative in itself.

Romance
You will make your partners feel wonderful, and be very forthcoming with romantic and flattering gifts. Your zest for sex will encourage and help relax the shyest of partners.

When angered, you will become a real lion – if in sheep's clothing. But any resentment or brooding after you have had your say would be most uncharacteristic. Magnanimity is always present, even if you are capable of reducing a rival or an enemy to a quivering jelly.

The Moon in Leo

Your well-being

The Leo body area is the spine: look
after it and exercise it. If you sit at an
office desk all day, get a backrest
chair. Because Leo also rules the
heart, any Arien sporting activity is
important, too. You are a wholehogger
and, with your Moon in a fire sign,
you could succumb to the Arien fault
of burning yourself out of both
physical and emotional energy.

Planning ahead

The Arien enterprising spirit is a very
necessary asset for you, since you
really love luxury and expensive

quality. You are often attracted to
things that are well beyond your price
range. If you are enterprising,
creative, work hard, and make large
amounts of money, you will achieve
great inner fulfilment.

Parenthood

You will be a loving, if somewhat
domineering, parent. If you curb the
latter trait, you will be a great source
of inspiration to your children, giving
them every encouragement. Even
when you have no alternative but to
criticize them, you will do so in such a
way as to encourage their efforts.

THE MOON IN
VIRGO

THE ARIEN NEED FOR ACTION BLENDS WELL WITH VIRGO'S
QUICK BUT CAREFUL RESPONSES TO SITUATIONS. YOU
WILL BE FAR LESS LIKELY TO MAKE SILLY MISTAKES THAN OTHER
PEOPLE OF YOUR SUN SIGN.

Your Moon in Virgo, which is an earth sign, gives your character a dimension that is very much in contrast to your fire sign Arien Sun.

Self-expression
While having the typical quick Arien grasp of a situation, you respond not only practically but also very analytically, seeing every loophole. Try not to become damningly critical of other people, for a very understandable tendency not to suffer fools gladly can go a bit too far at times, especially when Arien hasty action meets with Virgoan fussiness.

You are among the most practical of Ariens, being capable of either theoretical or active work, but may not be terribly patient. Take a break rather than struggling on to the point where you want to give up.

Although Ariens are certainly not celebrated for their shyness, it is just possible that in some way you have

had to come to terms with a degree of reticence. Maybe it has inhibited you in just one area of your life, perhaps as the result of critical put-downs from your parents when you were young. Your Virgoan modesty could have predominated until the positive force of Aries came into its own.

Romance
Your Arien emotion is dampened by the qualities of your Moon sign. It will lead you to think sensibly before overwhelming your partner with passion. When you are annoyed you may tend to carp and nag, but you will rarely be resentful.

Your well-being
The Virgoan body area is the stomach. You need an above-average amount of fibre, and might respond well to a vegetarian diet. The Moon in Virgo can also cause a considerable build-up of tension: many Sun sign Virgoans

The Moon in Virgo

suffer from migraine, and because Aries rules the head and makes its subjects prone to bad headaches, you could sometimes succumb to them. Find a way to counter stress; note its early symptoms, and try to distance yourself from any problem. This is vital if you are to remain productive.

Planning ahead

Ariens are generous; Virgoans, on the whole, are not. There is clearly a potential conflict between the two. If

it is troublesome, then you would be wise to simply tell the Virgoan level of your personality where it can go.

Parenthood

All Ariens have the capacity to enjoy parenthood, but be careful that you are not more critical towards your children than you realize. They could easily take you much more seriously than you might imagine. If they do, make it up to them with some special treats to show how sorry you are.

THE MOON IN
LIBRA

ARIES AND LIBRA ARE POLAR OR OPPOSITE SIGNS, WHICH MEANS
THAT YOU WERE BORN AT THE TIME OF THE FULL MOON.
ALWAYS GUARD AGAINST RESTLESSNESS, AND DO NOT ALLOW
INDECISION TO MAR YOUR ARIEN ENTHUSIASM.

A ll of us, in one way or another, tend to express certain attributes of our polar, or opposite, Zodiac sign. In your case, this is Libra, which is right across the Zodiac circle from Aries. Because the Moon happened to be in that sign when you were born, this polarity is expressed in a very interesting way: you will react to people with much greater consideration for their feelings than most people of your Sun sign.

Self-expression
You can be diplomatic and tactful, and when the going gets tough, you will recognize any negative symptoms of stress and really cut out and relax.

Having said that, most people born like you, at the time of the Full Moon, are prone to restlessness, and all too often harbour some kind of inner feeling of discontent. You must be on your guard against this. Perhaps you tend to change occupations rather

too often, and therefore never completely satisfy your sense of inner fulfilment. Examine your attitudes and opinions occasionally, as they may tend to be over-volatile or, conversely, stuck in a rut.

Romance
Your Libran Moon sign makes you diplomatic, far more tactful, and less hasty, than most Ariens. Libra is, emotionally, not a very powerfully charged sign. It is enhanced by fiery Arien warmth, while Arien sexual passion is softened by warm affection and a beautiful expression of romance. Any selfishness is considerably mitigated in you, although you may suffer twinges of resentment from time to time.

Your well-being
The Libran body area is the kidneys, and as a result of the polar lunar influence you may have slight kidney

The Moon in Libra

upsets. You could also suffer from many Arien headaches. No doubt you also find rich, expensive, and delicious food hard to resist. If you tend to put on weight easily, keep up the exercise and sporting activities, otherwise your gourmet interests may damage your figure.

Planning ahead

Your Libran Moon sign inclines you to luxury – something many Ariens are not too fussed about. But if you really do enjoy luxurious living, it is clear that you should exploit your enterprising qualities as much as you can. You will do well to be one of those Ariens who has two sources of income (apart from anything else, the variety will satisfy you).

Parenthood

You are an excellent parent, and will be sympathetic to your children's opinions; you will not want them to be clones of yourself. A hint of Libran indecisiveness could, however, be irritating for them at times.

THE MOON IN
SCORPIO

THE FIERY EMOTION OF ARIES AND THE INTENSE EMOTION OF
SCORPIO BUILD POWERFUL RESOURCES ON WHICH TO DRAW
DURING HARD TIMES. BE CAREFUL THAT JEALOUSY DOES NOT
SPOIL YOUR ARIEN STRAIGHTFORWARDNESS.

There is a long-standing tradition that links Aries with Scorpio: both were ruled by Mars until the discovery of Pluto. After considerable discussion, Pluto was placed as the ruler of Scorpio.

Self-expression

Your resources of emotional, as well as physical, energy are considerable. You have what it takes to achieve a great deal. If you really concentrate upon your objectives, you will express your potential to the full. But if you fail to do this, you are likely to suffer from an unpleasant sense of discontent.

A full, busy, rewarding life, and a deep involvement in both work and spare-time activities is what you need. Stagnation is your great enemy. You have a liking for mystery, ranging from detective fiction to the occult. If you feel attracted to the latter, or think you have a psychic side to your nature, do not play around with

seances or Ouija boards. Seek sound professional advice from someone who is regarded as trustworthy.

Romance

Your need for sexual fulfilment is above average. Make sure that you find a partner who is sympathetic to your demanding needs, and who is as lively as you are.

Your deep and passionate emotions mean that you can respond to certain situations with a show of jealousy and, perhaps, possessiveness. Your suspicions may well be unfounded, so be careful how you express them.

Your well-being

The traditional Scorpio body area is the genitals. "Safe sex" may therefore prove to be more essential for you than it is for most people.

With this Sun and Moon combination, your physical energy level is very high, so exercise is

The Moon in Scorpio

terribly important to you. One of your important activities should be sporting – all kinds of swimming are excellent for you, and do not ignore your Arien competitive spirit, spiked with Scorpio emotions.

Planning ahead

As long as you control your Arien enthusiasm when faced with get-rich-quick schemes you are usually very shrewd when dealing with money. Use your intuition to discover weaknesses and foresee problems. In general, you should invest in big companies with steady growth.

Parenthood

You will be an excellent parent, but try not to force your own interests on your children, since you may tend to dominate them. Your psychological and emotional energy is infectious. By all means let it affect your children, and be proud of their progress, but allow them to be themselves.

THE MOON IN
SAGITTARIUS

YOU RESPOND TO SUGGESTIONS AND CHALLENGES IMMEDIATELY
AND WITH A NATURAL ENTHUSIASM. SINCE ARIES AND
SAGITTARIUS ARE FIRE SIGNS, YOU MAY HAVE TO DEVELOP YOUR
STAMINA, OR YOUR PROJECTS COULD EASILY FIZZLE OUT.

You are well blessed; an Arien Sun and a Sagittarian Moon is an extremely positive combination. With your straightforward attitude to life you are well able to assess problems, and to put them into a coherent perspective.

Self-expression
Your powerful fire element prompts you to live a full life, but it does not encourage you to cope with detail. Your boredom level is very low, and can lead you to cast aside a project or ambition just because something else seems more attractive.

You are somewhat overly optimistic, and disappointments can spread a layer of gloom over your life. Still, this should not last – soon you will be off on another venture. You do need variety in your activities, perhaps involving moving from a physically demanding project to one that exercises your brain.

Try, however, to develop consistency of effort and a little more patience. You are more versatile than most Ariens but, to avoid exhaustion, should make sure that you set aside time each day for relaxation and contemplation. Some of your deepest instincts incline you to a philosophic approach to life, and to an interest in esoteric subjects, like religion.

Romance
You are a lively, passionate lover whose many delightful ways will endear you to a partner. There will, however, be an element of duality in your nature that could create some rather tricky situations. You should also guard against a tendency to be off-hand with people.

Your well-being
The Arien body area covers the hips and thighs. Arien women with a Sagittarian Moon will tend to put on

The Moon in Sagittarius

weight in these areas quite as readily as their Sagittarian Sun sign sisters. The Sagittarian body organ is the liver. If you like rich casseroles, rather heavy food, and red wine, you would therefore be wise to keep a hangover cure at the ready.

Take care that undue haste does not lead to you incurring long-lasting sports injuries.

Planning ahead

You are very prone to risk-taking. When you are confronted by a challenge, you will respond almost instantaneously. Be careful, since this could be foolhardy. Get-rich-quick schemes could have an almost irresistible attraction, and you may have a rather strong gambling streak.

Parenthood

You could scarcely be a more lively and enthusiastic parent, but because you will be so keen for your children to progress in life, you might find it difficult to adjust to a child with a slower pace of progress than you would like. Try to be patient, and make sure that you take enough time out to listen to your children carefully and sympathetically.

THE MOON IN
CAPRICORN

YOUR PRACTICAL CAPRICORNIAN MOON WILL ENCOURAGE YOU TO
ACHIEVE ARIEN OBJECTIVES. TO BE FIRST IS IN YOUR
NATURE. CONFRONTED WITH CHALLENGES, YOUR REACTION IS
AMBITIOUS: YOU ASPIRE TO REACH THE TOP.

You take life more seriously than any other Moon sign Capricornians. This does not, however, mean that your outlook will be negative. The Moon in Capricorn gives you a marvellously off-beat sense of humour.

Self-expression
Your Arien desire to be first will be encouraged by the Capricornian ambition to "climb every mountain". You will not only reach the top, but you could also be the first of your peer group to do so.

Oddly enough, given your Arien assertiveness and Capricornian instinct for progress, doubts will creep in from time to time when you are confronted with challenges. This is most likely if your parents were at all domineering or unsympathetic. Counter such uncertainties by recalling that you are a free agent, and have what it takes to win out.

Romance
Emotionally, Capricorn is a cool sign, so your Arien passion will be kept well under control, and carefully directed. You may find it easier to be faithful to a lover than many people of your Sun sign. You may also tend to respond well to partners who are either wealthier than you or seem to be of a superior social class. This may not always be a good thing.

Because Capricorn is an earth sign, you possess plenty of practical caution. Do not allow this to dampen your pleasure when it comes to love.

Your well-being
The Capricornian body area is the knees and shins. Capricornians are prone to stiffness in the joints, so rheumatic pains and arthritic conditions are not unknown to them. These ailments are less likely to afflict you if you exercise. If, however, you should sustain an injury while

The Moon in Capricorn

exercising, especially to your knees, go to a physiotherapist at once. Otherwise long-term damage or cartilage problems may occur. Most Ariens find it easy to keep up sporting and exercise regimes, and exercise is just as important for you as it is for those with different Moon signs.

Planning ahead

Caution and a practical instinct will act in your favour where financial and career matters are concerned. While, as an Arien, you will like striding forward, and perhaps taking risks, with the Moon in Capricorn you will prefer a carefully regulated pace, both in climbing the career ladder and in increasing your bank balance.

Parenthood

You will want only the best for your children. Be careful, however, about working extra hours, or bringing work home in order to provide materially for your children. Make sure that you take time to enjoy their company and to have fun with them.

THE MOON IN
AQUARIUS

THE MOON IN AQUARIUS IS INVENTIVE, ORIGINAL, GLAMOROUS,
AND COOL, WHILE ARIES IS WARM AND PASSIONATE. BE AN
INDIVIDUALIST, BUT TRY NOT TO LET YOUR AQUARIAN MOON
DISTANCE YOU FROM YOUR ARIEN QUALITIES.

You are among the most inventive of Ariens, and are capable of having really original ideas. What is more, you have the enthusiasm to bring these ideas to fruition. Your potential is great, and should not be ignored or suppressed.

Self-expression
Aries is a sign needing considerable independence, and Aquarius is the most independent sign in the Zodiac. It is therefore hardly surprising that you like to do things your own way, and will respond very negatively to anyone who tries to boss you about or cramp your style. You have of necessity to learn by your own mistakes, even if this means doing things the hard way.

Because Aquarius is of the fixed quality, you could well surprise others by reacting very stubbornly at times. You will also have a tendency to be unpredictable, which can often be appealing. Be careful, however, that this trait does not go hand in hand with Aquarian selfishness.

Romance
Because of your Aquarian Moon, you may tend to rationalize your emotions, or even to detach yourself from them, especially during the early stages of an emotional relationship. But there is also a very romantic side to your Aquarian Moon, and an instinctive liking for glamour. These traits will inevitably colour your attitudes.

An overall need for independence may mean that you put off forming a permanent relationship or marriage until quite late in life. Your love and sex life will, however, have the usual exuberance of Aries.

Your well-being
Aquarius rules the ankles and the circulation. You could feel the cold rather more than most Sun sign

The Moon in Aquarius

Ariens, and it is important that you keep your circulation in good order. If you are able to keep active, you should also avoid developing stiffness in the joints, something to which Aquarians are rather prone.

Planning ahead
The Aquarian attraction to the glamorous and romantic often creates a desire for expensive, rather glitzy things, unusual objects for the home, and expensive and original clothes

and perfumes. It is here that Arien enthusiasm could encourage you to spend an excessive amount of money.

Parenthood
You should not find it difficult to keep up with your children's crazes. At times, you may even overtake them in this respect; you should have no problem with the generation gap. Do, however, control any tendency to be unpredictable, since children like to know where they stand.

THE MOON IN
PISCES

BY COMBINING YOUR FIERY ARIEN QUALITIES WITH THE PISCEAN
SENSITIVITY OF YOUR EMOTIONAL REACTIONS
TO SITUATIONS, YOU WILL MAKE THE MOST OF THESE VIVIDLY
CONTRASTING CHARACTERISTICS.

Aries is often said to be the pioneer of the Zodiac, and Pisces the poet, so it is not surprising that you are an individual with contrasting sides to your personality.

Self-expression

Your Arien Sun gives you all the positive, forthright qualities that are associated with the sign. In fact, it could eclipse the influence of your sensitive, intuitive Moon. You may sometimes lack Arien self-confidence when confronted with a challenge. Have you a deep-rooted tendency to shy away from some situations?

Looking at this combination in another way, it is likely that you are far more caring and sympathetic than many Ariens. You will certainly spend time, energy, and money helping other people, and this could occasionally leave you feeling drained. You could well be creative, in a variety of ways. Your Piscean instinct

will incline you to want to work behind the scenes, while your Arien Sun will want you to be out in front.

Romance

Your fiery Arien emotion is combined with the emotion of Pisces, which is a water sign. This makes you a caring lover, sensitive to your partner's needs. Beware, however, of a negative Piscean trait: deceptiveness. This is often brought on by a tendency to take the easy way out of situations.

Your well-being

The Piscean body area is the feet. You may hate the restriction of wearing shoes, especially high-heeled shoes, and going barefoot will therefore have its attraction. But remember the Arien tendency to be accident prone, which could mean that you are easily susceptible to cut and grazed feet, and bunions or veruccas. You may not enjoy the

The Moon in Pisces

rough and tumble of the types of sport that Ariens usually like. Bearing in mind your Arien strength and vitality, however, you could well be attracted to gymnastics when you are young, and to any kind of dancing. This, and perhaps ice skating, should be particularly good for you.

Planning ahead

Enthusiasm, the inability to take a hard line, and a tendency to be impractical, could make you liable to fall for risky schemes. If, like many Ariens, you have an enterprising streak, it is possible that you may need a business partner to steady you and keep an eye on the books. Beware, too, of over-investment.

Parenthood

You will be sensitive to your children's needs, but may tend to worry rather too much about them – more, in fact, than most other Ariens. Instead of allowing your admirable Piscean imagination to invent all sorts of catastrophes that may have happened to your children, use this imagination in devising your own bedtime stories to enthral them. You will not find this difficult.

MOON CHARTS

THE FOLLOWING TABLES WILL ENABLE YOU TO DISCOVER YOUR
MOON SIGN. THEN, BY REFERRING TO THE PRECEDING
PAGES, YOU WILL BE ABLE TO INVESTIGATE ITS QUALITIES, AND
SEE HOW THEY WORK WITH YOUR SUN SIGN.

By referring to the Moon charts opposite and overleaf, look up the year of your birth and the Zodiacal glyph for your birth month. Refer next to the Moon Table (*below, left*) in which the days of the month are listed against a number. The number against the day of the month in which you were born indicates how many Zodiacal glyphs (*below, right*) must be

counted before you reach your Moon sign. You may have to count to Pisces and return to Aries. For example, given the birthdate 21 May 1991, you initially need to find the Moon sign for the first day of May in that year. It is Sagittarius (♐). With the birthdate falling on the 21st, nine signs must be added. The Moon sign for this birth date is therefore Virgo (♍).

MOON TABLE

DAYS OF THE MONTH AND NUMBER OF
SIGNS THAT SHOULD BE ADDED

DAY	ADD	DAY	ADD	DAY	ADD	DAY	ADD
1	0	9	4	17	7	25	11
2	1	10	4	18	8	26	11
3	1	11	5	19	8	27	12
4	1	12	5	20	9	28	12
5	2	13	5	21	9	29	1
6	2	14	6	22	10	30	1
7	3	15	6	23	10	31	2
8	3	16	7	24	10		

ZODIACAL GLYPHS

♈	Aries
♉	Taurus
♊	Gemini
♋	Cancer
♌	Leo
♍	Virgo
♎	Libra
♏	Scorpio
♐	Sagittarius
♑	Capricorn
♒	Aquarius
♓	Pisces

	1923	1924	1925	1926	1927	1928	1929	1930	1931	1932	1933	1934	1935
JAN	♊	♏	♈	♌	♐	♈	♍	♑	♉	♎	♓	♋	♏
FEB	♌	♐	♉	♍	♑	♊	♏	♓	♋	♐	♈	♌	♑
MAR	♌	♑	♉	♍	♒	♋	♏	♓	♋	♐	♉	♍	♑
APR	♎	♓	♋	♏	♈	♍	♑	♉	♍	♒	♊	♎	♓
MAY	♏	♈	♌	♐	♉	♎	♒	♊	♎	♓	♋	♐	♈
JUN	♑	♉	♍	♒	♋	♏	♓	♌	♐	♉	♍	♑	♊
JUL	♒	♋	♏	♓	♌	♐	♈	♍	♑	♊	♎	♓	♋
AUG	♈	♌	♐	♉	♍	♒	♊	♏	♓	♋	♐	♈	♌
SEP	♉	♎	♒	♋	♏	♓	♌	♐	♈	♍	♑	♊	♎
OCT	♊	♏	♓	♌	♐	♉	♍	♑	♉	♎	♓	♋	♏
NOV	♌	♑	♉	♍	♑	♊	♏	♓	♋	♐	♈	♌	♑
DEC	♍	♒	♊	♎	♓	♌	♐	♈	♌	♑	♉	♍	♒

	1936	1937	1938	1939	1940	1941	1942	1943	1944	1945	1946	1947	1948
JAN	♈	♌	♑	♉	♍	♒	♊	♎	♓	♌	♐	♈	♍
FEB	♉	♎	♒	♊	♏	♈	♌	♐	♉	♍	♑	♊	♎
MAR	♊	♎	♒	♋	♐	♈	♌	♐	♉	♎	♒	♊	♏
APR	♌	♐	♈	♑	♉	♎	♒	♋	♏	♓	♌	♈	♑
MAY	♍	♑	♉	♎	♒	♊	♏	♓	♌	♐	♉	♍	♒
JUN	♎	♒	♋	♏	♈	♌	♑	♉	♎	♒	♊	♏	♓
JUL	♏	♈	♌	♑	♉	♍	♒	♊	♏	♓	♌	♐	♈
AUG	♑	♉	♎	♒	♋	♏	♈	♌	♐	♉	♍	♑	♊
SEP	♓	♋	♏	♈	♌	♑	♉	♍	♒	♋	♏	♓	♌
OCT	♈	♌	♑	♉	♎	♒	♊	♎	♓	♌	♐	♈	♍
NOV	♊	♎	♒	♊	♏	♈	♌	♐	♉	♍	♑	♊	♏
DEC	♋	♏	♓	♌	♑	♉	♍	♑	♊	♎	♒	♋	♐

	1949	1950	1951	1952	1953	1954	1955	1956	1957	1958	1959	1960	1961
JAN	♑	♊	♎	♓	♋	♏	♈	♌	♑	♉	♍	♒	♋
FEB	♓	♋	♐	♈	♍	♑	♉	♎	♒	♊	♏	♈	♌
MAR	♓	♋	♐	♉	♍	♑	♊	♏	♓	♋	♏	♈	♌
APR	♉	♍	♒	♊	♎	♓	♋	♐	♈	♌	♑	♊	♎
MAY	♊	♎	♓	♋	♐	♈	♍	♑	♉	♎	♒	♋	♏
JUN	♌	♐	♈	♍	♑	♊	♎	♓	♋	♐	♈	♌	♑
JUL	♍	♑	♊	♎	♓	♋	♏	♈	♌	♑	♉	♍	♒
AUG	♏	♓	♋	♐	♈	♍	♑	♉	♎	♒	♊	♏	♈
SEP	♐	♈	♍	♑	♊	♎	♒	♋	♐	♈	♌	♑	♊
OCT	♑	♊	♎	♓	♋	♏	♓	♌	♑	♉	♍	♒	♋
NOV	♓	♋	♏	♈	♍	♑	♉	♎	♒	♊	♏	♈	♌
DEC	♈	♌	♑	♊	♎	♒	♊	♏	♓	♌	♐	♉	♍

	1962	1963	1964	1965	1966	1967	1968	1969	1970	1971	1972	1973	1974
JAN	♏	♓	♌	♐	♈	♍	♑	♊	♎	♒	♋	♐	♈
FEB	♐	♉	♍	♒	♊	♏	♓	♋	♏	♈	♍	♑	♉
MAR	♐	♉	♎	♒	♊	♏	♈	♌	♐	♉	♍	♑	♊
APR	♒	♋	♏	♈	♌	♑	♉	♍	♒	♊	♏	♓	♋
MAY	♓	♌	♐	♉	♍	♒	♊	♎	♓	♋	♐	♈	♍
JUN	♉	♎	♒	♊	♏	♓	♌	♐	♉	♍	♑	♊	♎
JUL	♊	♏	♓	♌	♐	♈	♍	♑	♊	♎	♓	♋	♐
AUG	♌	♐	♉	♎	♒	♊	♏	♓	♋	♏	♈	♍	♑
SEP	♍	♒	♋	♏	♓	♋	♐	♉	♍	♑	♊	♎	♓
OCT	♏	♓	♌	♐	♈	♍	♒	♊	♎	♒	♋	♐	♈
NOV	♐	♉	♎	♒	♊	♎	♓	♋	♐	♈	♍	♑	♉
DEC	♑	♊	♏	♓	♋	♐	♈	♌	♑	♉	♎	♒	♊

58

	1975	1976	1977	1978	1979	1980	1981	1982	1983	1984	1985	1986	1987
JAN	♌	♑	♉	♍	♒	♊	♏	♓	♌	♐	♉	♍	♑
FEB	♎	♒	♋	♍	♈	♌	♐	♉	♍	♒	♊	♎	♓
MAR	♎	♓	♋	♍	♈	♍	♑	♉	♎	♒	♊	♏	♓
APR	♐	♈	♍	♑	♊	♎	♒	♋	♏	♈	♌	♑	♉
MAY	♑	♉	♎	♒	♋	♍	♓	♌	♐	♉	♍	♏	♊
JUN	♓	♋	♐	♈	♌	♑	♉	♎	♒	♊	♏	♓	♌
JUL	♈	♌	♑	♉	♍	♒	♋	♏	♓	♌	♐	♉	♍
AUG	♉	♎	♓	♋	♏	♈	♌	♐	♈	♎	♒	♊	♎
SEP	♋	♐	♈	♌	♐	♈	♎	♒	♊	♏	♓	♌	♐
OCT	♌	♑	♉	♍	♒	♋	♏	♓	♋	♐	♉	♍	♑
NOV	♎	♓	♋	♏	♓	♌	♐	♉	♍	♒	♊	♎	♓
DEC	♏	♈	♌	♐	♉	♍	♑	♊	♎	♓	♋	♐	♈

	1988	1989	1990	1991	1992	1993	1994	1995	1996	1997	1998	1999	2000
JAN	♊	♎	♒	♋	♏	♈	♌	♑	♉	♎	♒	♊	♏
FEB	♋	♐	♈	♍	♑	♉	♎	♒	♋	♍	♈	♌	♐
MAR	♌	♐	♉	♍	♒	♊	♎	♓	♋	♍	♈	♌	♐
APR	♍	♒	♊	♏	♓	♋	♐	♈	♍	♑	♊	♎	♓
MAY	♏	♓	♌	♐	♈	♍	♑	♉	♎	♒	♋	♏	♈
JUN	♐	♉	♍	♑	♊	♎	♓	♋	♐	♈	♌	♑	♉
JUL	♑	♊	♎	♒	♋	♐	♈	♌	♑	♉	♎	♒	♌
AUG	♓	♌	♐	♈	♍	♑	♉	♎	♓	♋	♏	♈	♎
SEP	♉	♍	♑	♊	♏	♓	♋	♏	♈	♌	♑	♉	♎
OCT	♊	♎	♒	♋	♐	♈	♌	♑	♉	♎	♒	♊	♏
NOV	♌	♐	♈	♍	♑	♉	♎	♒	♋	♏	♈	♌	♑
DEC	♍	♑	♉	♎	♒	♋	♏	♈	♌	♐	♉	♍	♒

THE SOLAR SYSTEM

THE STARS, OTHER THAN THE SUN, PLAY NO PART IN THE SCIENCE OF ASTROLOGY. ASTROLOGERS USE ONLY THE BODIES IN THE SOLAR SYSTEM, EXCLUDING THE EARTH, TO CALCULATE HOW OUR LIVES AND PERSONALITIES CHANGE.

Pluto
Pluto takes 246 years to travel around the Sun. It affects our unconscious instincts and urges, gives us strength in difficulty, and perhaps emphasizes any inherent cruel streak.

Neptune
Neptune stays in each sign for 14 years. At best it makes us sensitive and imaginative; at worst it encourages deceit and carelessness, making us worry.

Uranus
Uranus's influence can make us friendly, kind, eccentric, inventive, and unpredictable.

Saturn
In ancient times, Saturn was the most distant known planet. Its influence can limit our ambition and make us either overly cautious (but practical), or reliable and self-disciplined.

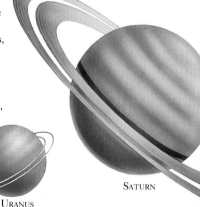

SATURN

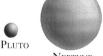

PLUTO

NEPTUNE

URANUS

Jupiter

Jupiter encourages expansion, optimism, generosity, and breadth of vision. It can, however, also make us wasteful, extravagant, and conceited.

Mars

Much associated with energy, anger, violence, selfishness, and a strong sex drive, Mars also encourages decisiveness and leadership.

JUPITER

The Moon

Although it is a satellite of the Earth, the Moon is known in astrology as a planet. It lies about 240,000 miles from the Earth and, astrologically, is second in importance to the Sun.

 MERCURY

THE MOON

VENUS

EARTH

MARS

The Sun

The Sun, the only star used by astrologers, influences the way we present ourselves to the world – our image or personality; the "us" we show to other people.

Venus

The planet of love and partnership, Venus can emphasize all our best personal qualities. It may also encourage us to be lazy, impractical, and too dependent on other people.

Earth

Every planet contributes to the environment of the Solar System, and a person born on Venus would no doubt be influenced by our own planet in some way.

Mercury

The planet closest to the Sun affects our intellect. It can make us inquisitive, versatile, argumentative, perceptive, and clever, but maybe also inconsistent, cynical, and sarcastic.